Foundation Level 2

Unit 4

Supplying Information for Management Control

British Library Cataloguing-in-Publication Data

A catalogue record for this book is available from the British Library.

Published by Foulks Lynch Ltd
Number 4
The Griffin Centre
Staines Road
Feltham
Middlesex
TW14 0HS

Phone: 020 8831 9990

Fax: 020 8831 9991

Email: info@foulkslynch.com

Why not visit our website today - www.foulkslynch.com

ISBN 0 7483 4702 X

© Foulks Lynch Ltd, 2001

All rights reserved. No part of this publication may be reproduced, stored in a retrieval system, or transmitted, in any form or by any means, electronic, mechanical, photocopying, recording or otherwise, without the prior written permission of Foulks Lynch Ltd.

Contents

Chapter		Page
Preface		iv
1	Introduction to cost accounting	1
2	Classification of costs and cost behaviour	4
3	Coding of costs and income	10
4	Materials costs	13
5	Labour costs	16
6	Expenses	20
7	The selling function	23
8	Data presentation	24
9	Collecting information	32
10	Basic budgeting and standard costing	35
11	Comparisons of information	38
12	Reporting	41
Index		45

Preface

This is the first edition of the AAT Unit 4 Lynchpin.

Lynchpins cover the syllabus thoroughly, complementing the Textbook coverage. They are not just a checklist of topics to learn but rather cover the key points with succinct detail that will bring the topics back to the front of your mind. Diagrams and worked examples all help the revision process and focal points concentrate the mind on key areas of examination technique. The books are fully indexed, for easy reference.

The books are pocket sized - but they pack a big punch - any time - anywhere.

Email: info@foulkslynch.com

Why not visit our website today – www.foulkslynch.com

CHAPTER 1 INTRODUCTION TO COST ACCOUNTING

1 Management information

- Management information, the product of management information systems, includes both financial, cost and management accounting aspects of a business entity.

2 Financial accounting

- Definition
  - the classification and recording of monetary transactions; and
  - the presentation and interpretation of the results of those transactions in order to assess performance over a period and the financial position at a given date.

3 Cost accounting

- Definition

  The establishment of budgets, standard costs and actual costs of operations, processes, activities or products, and the analysis of variances, profitability or the social use of funds.

4 Management accounting

- Definition

  An integral part of management concerned with identifying, presenting and interpreting information.

- Used for
  - formulation of strategy
  - planning and controlling activities
  - decision taking
  - optimising the use of resources
  - disclosure to shareholders and others external to the entity
  - disclosure to employees

Notes

SUPPLYING INFORMATION FOR MANAGEMENT CONTROL

- safeguarding assets.

5 Benefits of cost accounting

- ❑ The 'value added' from systems including:
  - discloses profitable and unprofitable activities
  - identifies waste and inefficiency
  - analyses movements in profits
  - estimates and fixes prices
  - values stocks
  - develops budgets
  - evaluates policy decisions.

6 The purpose of management information

- ❑ Management information is used by managers as an aid to:
  - decision making
  - planning
  - control.

7 Responsibility accounting

- ❑ A responsibility centre is a segment of an organisation whose manager is accountable for a specified set of activities
- ❑ Responsibility accounting is a system where the plans or budgets for each responsibility centre are compared with the actual level achieved, and explanations are sought for any discrepancies.

8 Cost centres

- ❑ A cost centre is a department or other clearly identifiable part of the business for which costs may be collected. Examples include:
  - accountancy firm - the audit department
  - hotel - the restaurant

9 Cost units

❑ A cost unit is a unit of the product or service for which costs may be ascertained. Examples include:

- brickmaking   -   1,000 bricks
- passenger transport   -   Passenger/kilometres

10 Profit centres

❑ A profit centre is a department or other clearly identifiable part of the business whose costs and revenues can be ascertained.

11 Investment centres

❑ An investment centre is a department or other clearly identifiable part of the business for which costs, revenues and investment can be ascertained.

CHAPTER 2 CLASSIFICATION OF COSTS AND COST BEHAVIOUR

1 Cost classification

- Cost classification is the logical grouping of similar costs, so that they may be accumulated to produce useful information. There are many different cost classifications, for example those described below.

- Classification by behaviour as the activity level changes. Costs can be fixed, variable, step or semi-variable.

- Classification by element. This identifies costs as being either materials, labour or expenses.

- Classification by direct/indirect costs. Direct costs are those costs which can be identified with the cost unit to which they relate eg, the raw material used in making a piece of furniture. Direct materials, direct labour and direct expenses together make prime cost.

- Indirect costs are overheads eg, indirect labour, material and expenses, which cannot be directly allocated to a cost centre or cost unit.

- Classification by function. Costs are identified by the function of the business responsible for incurring them eg, production, sales, administration.

- Classification by normal/abnormal costs. This classification enables exception reporting to be used: normal costs are those which are expected, the exceptions are abnormal costs.

- Classification by controllable/non-controllable costs. This enables costs to be reported to the manager who controls them. It is important when evaluating managers, to include only costs which they can control.

- Classification by relevance. Relevant costs are those which are charged by the decision maker's choice of action. Irrelevant costs are those which are unaffected by the decision.

2 Analysis of costs

❑ Costs may be analysed between those which are fixed ie, unaffected by activity changes, and those which are variable ie, which change in proportion to activity changes.

❑ The following graphs illustrate total fixed costs and fixed cost per unit.

Graphs showing relationship between rent and output in total

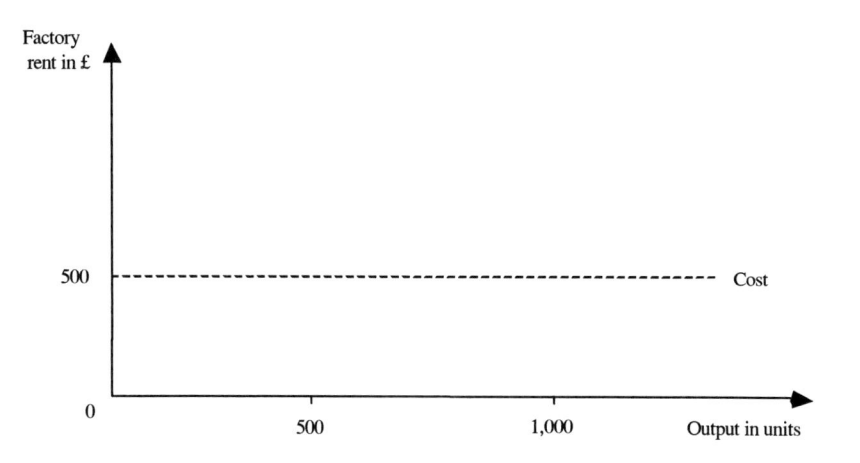

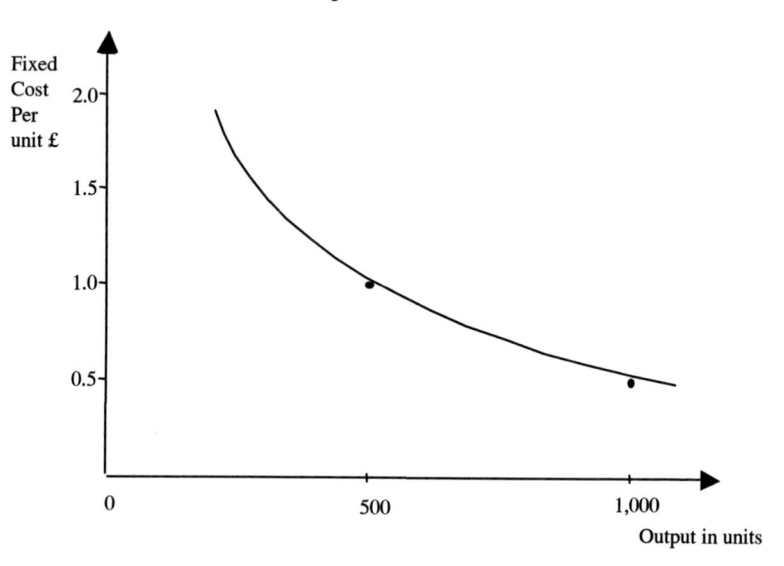

SUPPLYING INFORMATION FOR MANAGEMENT CONTROL

per unit

```
Fixed
Cost    2.0
Per
unit £
        1.5

        1.0

        0.5


         0           500              1,000
                                  Output in units
```

CHAPTER 2 CLASSIFICATION OF COSTS AND COST BEHAVIOUR

❑ The following graphs illustrate total variable costs and variable cost per unit.

Graph showing relationship between raw material, cost and output in total

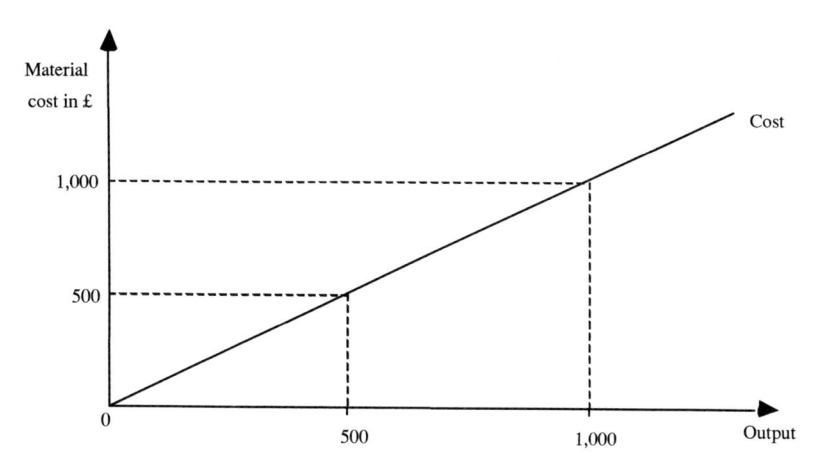

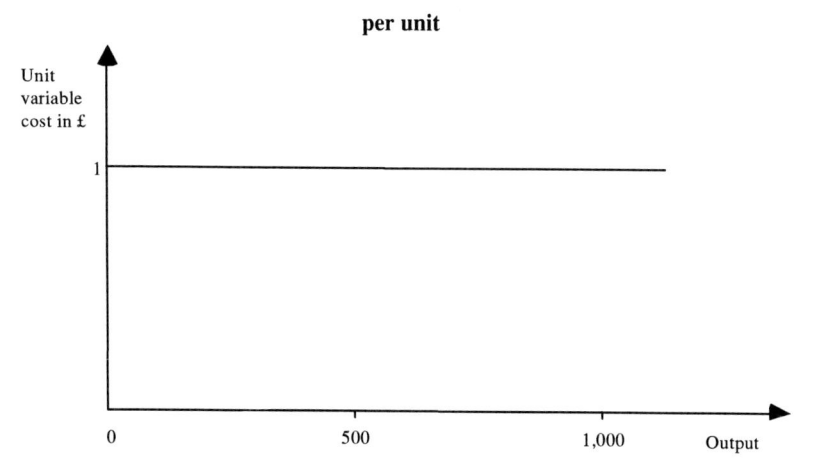

(Graph: Material cost in £ on vertical axis, Output on horizontal axis. A straight line labelled "Cost" rises from the origin through (500, 500) and (1,000, 1,000).)

per unit

(Graph: Unit variable cost in £ on vertical axis, Output on horizontal axis. A horizontal line at £1 extends across the range of output up to 1,000.)

- The relevant range of activity represents the range of activity levels within which an organisation would be expected to operate. Within these ranges the cost/activity relationship tends to be linear, even if it is not linear outside the relevant range.

- Many variable costs change per unit if we move out of the relevant range.

Graph showing relationship between the total cost of tyres and the output of cars

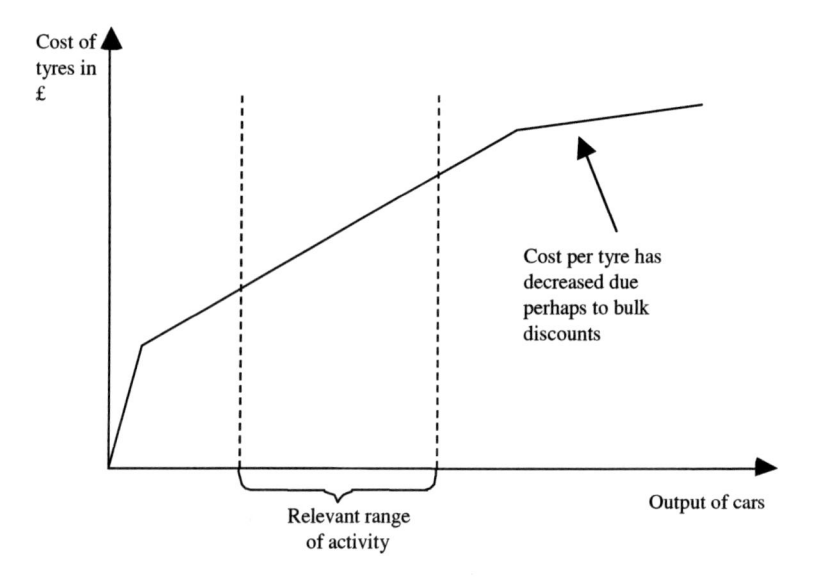

[Graph: x-axis "Output of cars", y-axis "Cost of tyres in £". A curve rises steeply from the origin, then continues at a moderate linear slope through the "Relevant range of activity" (marked by dashed vertical lines), then flattens at higher output levels. An arrow points to the flatter section with the annotation: "Cost per tyre has decreased due perhaps to bulk discounts".]

- Many fixed costs are step costs if we move out of the relevant range.

Graph showing relationship between total rent and output

Step costs

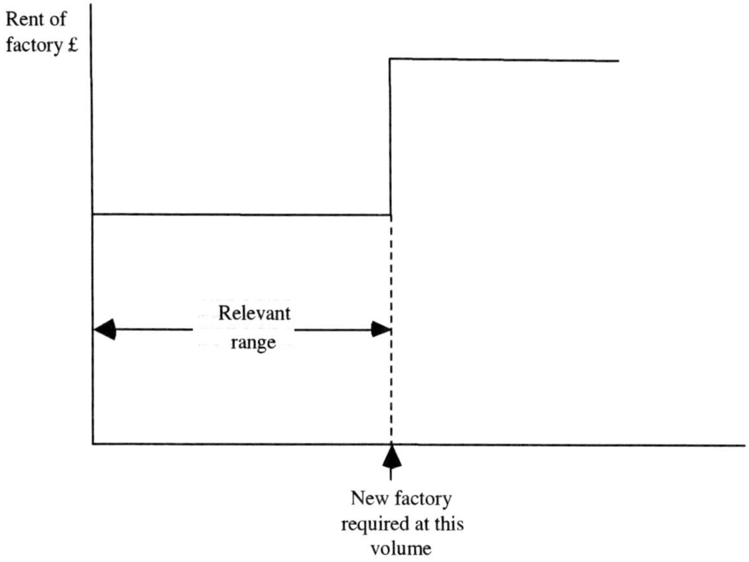
Rent of
factory £
Relevant
range
New factory
required at this
volume

CHAPTER 3 CODING OF COSTS AND INCOME

1 Cost codes

❑ Definition

A code is a system of symbols designed to be applied to a classified set of items, to give a brief accurate reference, facilitating entry to the records, collation and analysis.

2 Code structure for costs

❑ The code structure for analysis of costs could include:

- cost centre code
- classification of cost
- type of cost.

eg, **Cost Centres**
    100

- machining   101
- finishing   102
- packing   103
- maintenance   104
- contract   105
- office   106

Classification of cost
    120

- direct   121
- indirect   122

Type of cost
    130

- material   131
- labour   132
- expense/overhead 133

An invoice for materials coded in production in the initial process would be coded as:

101/121/131
machining/direct/material

3 Code structure for sales

❑ Sales analysis/coding structure may comprise:

Sales areas			
200	•	North & Scotland	201
	•	Midlands	202
	•	South East	203
	•	South West	204

Product Groups			
210	•	'AB'	211
	•	'CD'	212
	•	'EF'	213
	•	'GH'	214

Sales Revenue
220

Thus a sale to a Birmingham customer for products in group 'GH' would be coded as:
202/214/220
Midlands/'GH'/Sales

4 Using codes in practice

❑ Some costs will be coded within the financial accounting system by an analysis of the expenditure at source ie, the purchase invoice.

❑ Other costs, such as labour, would be coded to cost centres and by job or process through an analysis of the payroll.

❑ Coding of the usage of material would be captured by an analysis of material requisitions.

Notes

SUPPLYING INFORMATION FOR MANAGEMENT CONTROL

- Types of sales income would be analysed by the coding of sales invoices.
- The design of the coding system would be influenced by the amount of detail required in the analysis of costs and revenue.

CHAPTER 4 MATERIAL COSTS

1 Types of material

❑ Items used in the manufacture of a product ie, raw materials are classified as direct material

❑ Consumable products used in production eg, oil

❑ Items used to operate the business eg, machine parts.

These are classified as indirect material ie, overhead.

2 Documents used to control the purchasing of materials

❑ Purchase requisition. Used to authorise the buyer to acquire a particular material. Usually issued by the stores department.

❑ Purchase order. Written by the buyer and sent to the supplier requesting them to deliver the goods ordered.

❑ Goods received note. Completed by the stores department to record receipt and condition of the goods from the supplier.

❑ Purchase invoice. The supplier will send an invoice requesting payment for the goods delivered.

3 Storekeeping

❑ Materials must be protected from deterioration, fire and theft.

❑ The best use must be made of the available space with a logical and tidy arrangement of different materials. If possible, items should be arranged so that:

- items are close to their point of use
- older stock is more accessible than new
- most frequently used items are easy to get
- items are clearly labelled
- items are packed in the quantities most frequently issued
- mechanical handling equipment can be used if possible.

Notes

SUPPLYING INFORMATION FOR MANAGEMENT CONTROL

- For control purposes:
  - the purchase order should be checked against the purchase requisition to ensure that only goods that are needed are ordered
  - the goods received should be checked against the purchase order (or purchase requisition) to ensure that only goods that have been ordered are accepted
  - the purchase invoice should be checked against the goods received note to ensure that only goods received are paid for.
- Centralised stores are single stores which are used to stock all items, whereas decentralised or sub-stores specialise in certain types of stock item.
- Advantages claimed for the use of decentralised sub-stores include:
  - reduction of material handling because items can be transported in bulk to a sub-store located close to where items are to be used
  - improved technical knowledge of the items stocked.
- Disadvantages of decentralised sub-stores include:
  - increases in numbers of staff
  - increases in the level of stock held
  - supervision/communication difficulties
- A bin is the storekeeping term for a location within the stores where a particular item is kept.
- A bin card is a record of the physical movement of items of a stock.

4 Use of materials

- Materials issued to production departments are controlled by a materials requisition.
- Returns of unused materials to store are recorded on a similar document.
- Transfers of materials from one department to another should also be evidenced in written documents.

Notes

5 Accounting for direct materials

❑ A stores ledger card is used to record all stock movements so that the value of the stock of each item can be calculated at any time.

❑ Perpetual inventory is the recording of transactions involving the movement of stock as they occur.

6 Attributing direct materials cost to production

❑ Materials are often purchased in large quantities at different prices, and then issued to production in small lots. It is impracticable to track the price of each physical item of stock as it is issued to production, and for costing purposes some kind of simplifying assumption must be made.

CHAPTER 5 LABOUR COSTS

1 Payroll

❏ Payroll preparation involves:

- calculating gross wages from time and activity records
- calculating net wages from PAYE and other deductions, and properly recording the deductions
- preparing an analysis of either total notes and coins to make up pay packets or payments to be made by the banking system.

❏ Physical security is important at all stages of payroll preparation and payment.

2 Functional analysis of wages

❏ Gross wages need to be analysed and posted to the cost accounts. This is simple if the time records coincide with the payment period (eg, in the case of weekly time sheets). But discrepancies will arise where this is not the case eg, where job sheets are used (because jobs will overlap pay weeks).

3 Remuneration methods

❏ The calculation of an employee's earnings can be based on different measures of activity.

- Time rates. This method pays employees an agreed rate per hour, with adjustments being made to this rate for overtime and unsociable hours. The difference between these enhanced rates and the normal rate is known as a premium. Incentive schemes encourage employees to work efficiently by providing them with a financial reward.

- Piecework. This method pays employees an agreed rate per unit produced. Care must be taken to ensure that piecework payment does not encourage quickly but poorly made products. Quality control checks must be made on the items produced before a worker is paid.

❏ Workers record their attendance times on time cards (such as gate cards or clock cards) as a basis for calculating their wages, and if applicable, for determining the costs to be charged to specific jobs or cost centres or units.

CHAPTER 5 LABOUR COSTS

- direct workers may also use job cards to record the time they spend on particular orders
- for piecework employees activity (or output) is usually recorded on a piecework ticket which shows the quantities of each item produced by the employee
- time-rate employees analyse their time to different activities or tasks using time sheets.

4 Incentive schemes

❑ Characteristics of good incentive schemes

- rewards are closely related to effort
- they are agreed by consultation between employer and employees
- they are understandable and simple to operate
- they are capable of being beneficial to the average worker.

❑ Premium bonus plans are based on payment of a basic time rate, plus a bonus based on the proportion of the time saved as compared to some agreed allowed time.

❑ In the Halsey scheme, the proportion is 50%, so bonus equals:

$$\frac{\text{Time allowed} - \text{Time taken}}{2} \times \text{Time rate}$$

❑ In the Rowan scheme the bonus is calculated as:

$$\text{Time worked} \times \frac{\text{Time allowed} - \text{Time taken}}{\text{Time allowed}} \times \text{Time rate}$$

❑ Example

Employee's basic rate is £6 per hour. The allowed time for Job X is 50 minutes. The time taken was 40 minutes.

Notes

SUPPLYING INFORMATION FOR MANAGEMENT CONTROL

The bonus under a Halsey scheme is:

$$\frac{50 \text{ minutes} - 40 \text{ minutes}}{2} \times 10\text{p per minute} = 50\text{p}$$

Under a Rowan scheme the bonus is:

$$40 \text{ minutes} \times \frac{50 \text{ minutes} - 40 \text{ minutes}}{50 \text{ minutes}} \times 10\text{p per minute} = 80\text{p}$$

Under either scheme, the bonus would be *in addition to* the basic rate for 40 minutes work, namely £4.

- Premium bonus plans may be appropriate for skilled craftsmen, but probably not for production line workers.

- Measured day work plans are based on the idea of increasing the basic rate of pay by a negotiated amount. The increase is based on the employee's past performance compared with an allowed time for particular jobs.

- Share of production plans is based on added value (ie, sales value of output less cost of external inputs). Increases in added value are shared between employer and employees, in that the employees receive a proportion (perhaps 40%) of the increase.

5 Techniques of incentive schemes

- The function of work study is to analyse, measure and value operations and processes. The results form the basis for operating incentive schemes, but will also assist in planning and control.

- Work study comprises three elements

  - method study
  - motion study
  - time study

Notes

CHAPTER 5 LABOUR COSTS

- Job evaluation is an attempt to provide a logical basis for paying different rates to different employees by assessing the characteristics of a job in comparison with other jobs.

- Merit rating is a system of evaluating the employee who is doing a particular job.

6 Labour cost accounting and reports

- Direct wages are those wage costs which can economically be identified with the cost unit.

- Indirect wages comprises the wage costs of indirect workers (eg, supervisors) plus the wages cost applicable to the time spent by direct workers on indirect tasks (eg, cleaning machines).

7 Overtime premium cost

- The cost of overtime premiums (ie, the excess paid above the normal hourly rate) must be analysed into its cause.

- If the overtime were worked at the specific request of the customer, then the cost of the overtime premium is a direct cost to the work for that customer. If it was not specifically requested by a customer, the overtime premium cost is an indirect cost.

8 Labour turnover

- Labour turnover is measured by calculating the ratio of the number of leavers in a period to the average workforce of the period.

- The objective is to minimise labour turnover in order to minimise the costs of recruiting and training replacement employees.

Notes

CHAPTER 6   EXPENSES

1   Coding, analysis and recording of expenses

❑ Introduction

To a cost accountant, there are three types of business expenditure: materials, labour and expenses.

❑ Definition

Expenses are all business costs that are not classified as materials or labour costs. The majority of expenses are indirect and thus overhead.

❑ Manufacturing expenses – example

Examples of expenses incurred during the manufacturing process are:

- the power for the machinery
- the lighting and heating of the factory
- general running costs of the machinery such as oil.

❑ Selling expenses – example

When selling goods to customers the expenses that might be incurred are:

- advertising costs
- packaging costs
- costs of delivering the goods to the customer.

❑ Administration expenses – example

The everyday running of the organisation will involve many different expenses including the following:

- rent of buildings
- business rates on buildings
- insurance of the buildings.

CHAPTER 6 EXPENSES

2 Cost centres and expenses - overheads

❑ Expenses can be either allocated or apportioned to a cost centre.

❑ Allocation is the allotment of whole items of cost to a cost centre or cost unit eg, indirect labour would be allocated to a cost centre through the coding system and its application in the analysis of the payroll.

❑ Apportionment is the allotment of proportions of items of cost to a cost centre or cost unit eg, heat and light would be apportioned on area occupied.

3 Capital and revenue expenditure

❑ Introduction

When a business spends money on an item it must be classified as either capital expenditure or revenue expenditure. The importance of the distinction between these two types of expenditure is in their accounting treatments, which are completely different.

❑ Capital expenditure

- Definition

  Capital expenditure is money spent by a business on fixed assets.

- Definition

  Fixed assets are assets of the business that are for long-term use in the business.

  When a business buys items of machinery, cars, computers, office furniture or a building these will all be classified as capital expenditure.

❑ Revenue expenditure

- Definition

  Revenue expenditure is all expenditure other than capital expenditure.

  Revenue expenditure will therefore include expenditure on materials, wages, power costs, lighting and heating bills, telephone bills, rent, to name but a few.

Notes

4 Depreciation

❑ Definition

Depreciation is the measure of the wearing out, consumption or other reduction in the useful economic life of a fixed asset.

- Straight line depreciation

    This is a method of charging the same amount of depreciation each year of the asset's life.

- Reducing balance method of depreciation

    The reducing balance method of depreciation applies a percentage depreciation rate to the net book value of the asset to calculate the annual depreciation charge.

CHAPTER 7 THE SELLING FUNCTION

1 Duties of the sales function

❑ The sales function of an organisation will typically be responsible for the following:

- processing orders from customers
- negotiating the details of the order
- notifying the production department of the order details
- preparing the despatch note for the goods
- preparing the sales invoice
- organising any necessary advertising.

2 The sales function as a cost or expense centre

❑ The costs of the function allocated and apportioned to the expense centre would include:

- labour eg, administration and sales salaries
- materials (these are indirect such as consumables and stationery)
- expenses or overheads eg, advertising, transport.

3 The sales function as a profit centre

❑ In addition to the above costs, if it were classed as a profit centre, then its management would be responsible for income from sales.

Notes

CHAPTER 8 DATA PRESENTATION

1 Presentation of data

❑ Data can be presented in the form of either:

- table
- diagram.

❑ The choice of presentation will depend upon:

- the nature and complexity of the data
- the user's needs
- method of presentation.

2 Tables

❑ Presenting data in a table often makes it much more clear.

- Definition

Tabulation is the systematic arrangement of numerical data to provide a logical account of the results of analysis.

- Rules of Tabulation

When preparing a tabulation the following factors need to be considered:

- Title
- Source
- Unit of Measure
- Headings
- Totals
- Percentages and ratios
- Column layout
- Simplicity
- Layout
- User needs.

❑ Example

Tennis Skill Ltd

Budget and actual labour costs per cost centre for January 20X1.

• *Cost Centres*	*Budget* £	*Actual* £	£ *(Increase/ decrease)*
Machining			
Direct Labour	6,500	6,400	100
Indirect Labour	2,100	2,150	(50)
Finishing			
Direct Labour	7,300	7,350	(50)
Indirect Labour	1,200	1,150	50
Packing			
Direct Labour	6,300	6,275	25
Indirect Labour	1,100	1,050	50
Total Labour Cost	£24,500	£24,375	£125

SOURCE: Budget manual and payroll analysis

3 Diagrammatic representation of data

❑ This is the form of either

- graph
- diagram

❑ Construction of graphs and diagrams

Principles to be followed are:

- all diagrams (and graphs) must have a title
- the source of data must be stated
- the units of measurement that have been used must be given
- the scale must be stated

- the axes must be clearly labelled
- neatness is essential.

❑ **Advantages of diagrams and graphs**

If these principles are followed than a diagram will have several advantages over a table:

- it is easier to understand than the mass of figures from a table
- relationships between figures are shown more clearly
- a quick, lasting and accurate impression is given of the significant and pertinent facts.

❑ **Types of diagram**

There are various methods of representing data diagrammatically. The first set of methods to be considered is

- pictograms
- bar charts – simple, component and multiple
- pie charts.

Each of these is considered in turn with examples to illustrate the method of construction.

Pictograms are, as the name implies, pictures (or symbols) which can readily be associated with the data under consideration.

Example

The following pictogram represents the car sales for International Cars plc for the three consecutive years 20X1 to 20X3:

Car sales 20X1 to 20X3

20X1
20X2
20X3
= 1 million cars
Source
Final accounts,
International Cars plc

- Bar Charts
  - simple bar chart

Example

The following bar chart represents the production of wheat in the UK for the years 20X1 to 20X3:

Wheat production UK, 20X1 to 20X3

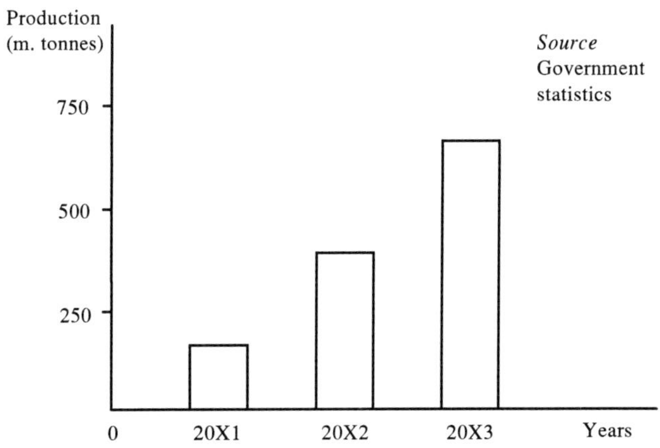
Production
(m. tonnes)
750
500
250
0
20X1
20X2
20X3
Years
Source
Government
statistics

- component bar chart

A component bar chart is drawn when each total figure is built up from several component parts.

Example

The following bar chart represents the grain production (rye, barley and wheat) in the UK for the years 20X4 to 20X6

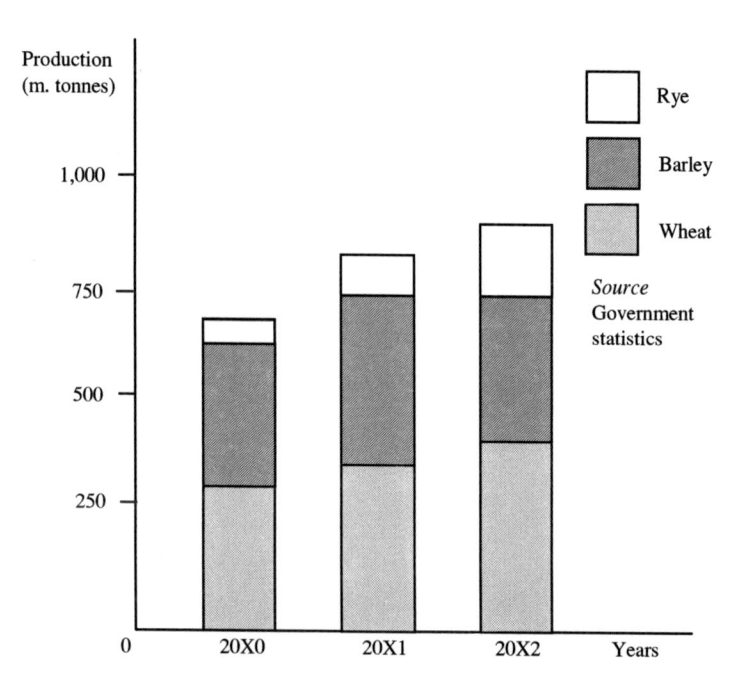

Source Government statistics

- multiple bar chart

This is drawn where two or more related items are compared. The bars are placed next to each other and each represents a different item.

CHAPTER 8 DATA PRESENTATION

Example

The following bar chart represents the sales of root vegetables (turnips, carrots and parsnips) in Scot Farms for the years 20X0 to 20X2:

Root vegetables 20X0 to 20X2

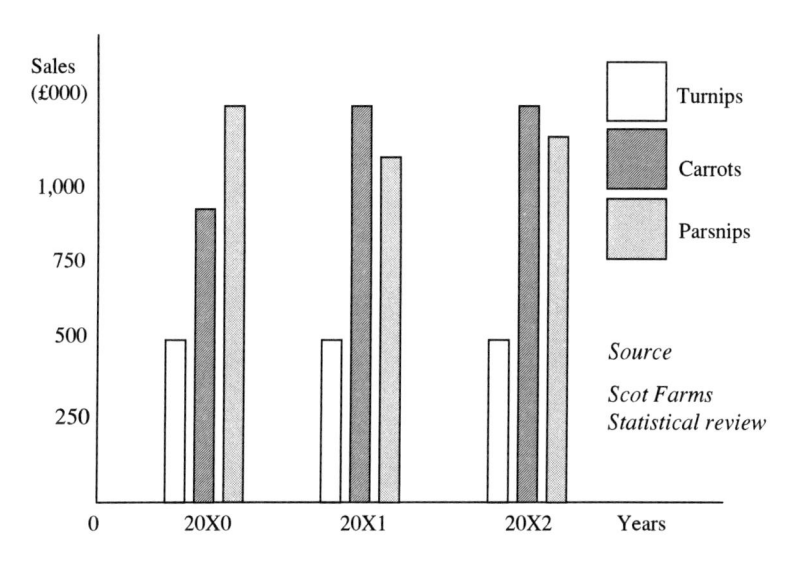

Source

Scot Farms Statistical review

Pie charts

These are usually drawn when the proportions of each class to the whole is important rather than the absolute value of each class. A circle is drawn, and divided into sectors such that the area of each sector is proportionate to the size of the figure represented. They are analogous to the component bar chart.

**Analysis of cost of production
Tennis Skill Ltd 20X0**

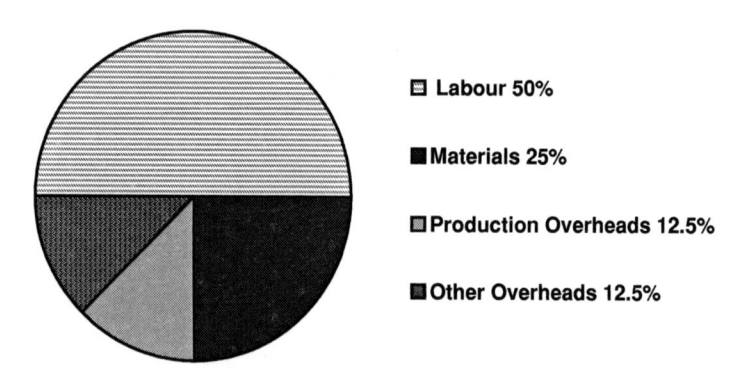

- Labour 50%
- Materials 25%
- Production Overheads 12.5%
- Other Overheads 12.5%

4 Use of computers

- Most spreadsheet packages have a facility for producing charts and diagrams.

5 Presentation of data in a graph

- There are a number of factors to consider when producing a graph:
  - title
  - axes of a graph
  - scales of the axes
  - starting point of the axis
  - plotting the graph.

Example

The following data is to be plotted on a graph:

Monthly sales

Month	£
January	6,800
February	7,200
March	5,600
April	6,900
May	7,500
June	8,000

Draw a graph to illustrate this information.

Solution

Monthly sales

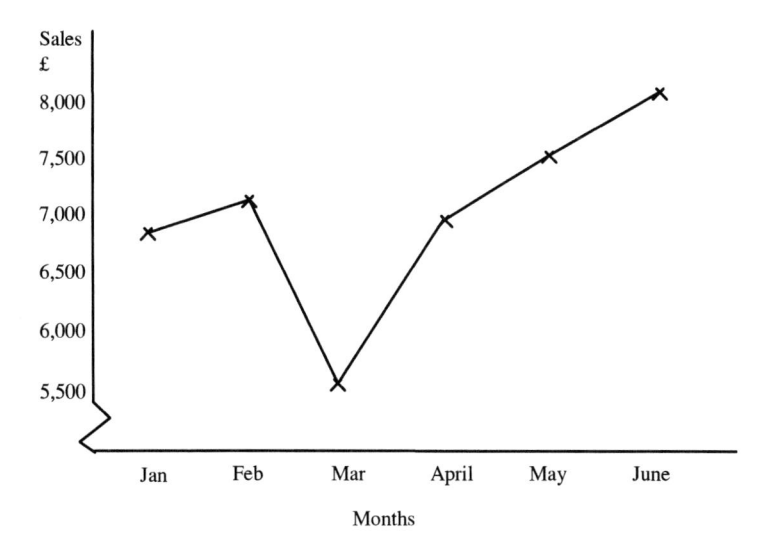

CHAPTER 9 COLLECTING INFORMATION

1 Cost bookkeeping

❑ Introduction

There are two main cost bookkeeping systems that a business might use:

- interlocking accounts
- integrated accounts

For this syllabus we will concentrate on interlocking cost accounts.

❑ Interlocking cost accounts

Definition

Interlocking accounts are a system in which the cost accounts are distinct from the financial accounts, the two sets of accounts being kept continuously in agreement by the use of control accounts.

The system maintains a cost ledger control account and a control account for stores, wages and salaries, production overheads, selling, distribution and administrative overheads.

2 Stores ledger control

When materials are purchased and analysed within the coding system as direct or indirect materials, they are debited to the stores ledger control and credited to the cost ledger control.

When issues are made, they are coded to either the cost centre using the material or by nature of the function requiring the material.

eg, Tennis Skill Ltd receive invoices in January 20X1 from suppliers of both direct and indirect materials for £45,000. The balance of stores on hand was £7,500. An analysis of material requisitions showed for January 20X1:

- Direct materials issued to production   £34,500
- Indirect materials used   £4,200
- Stationery used in selling function   £500

Cost control accounts would show

Cost ledger control

	£		£
		January	
		Stores ledger Control	45,000

Stores ledger control

	£		£
January Balance b/f	7,500	January	
Cost Ledger Control	45,000	W-I-P (direct materials)	34,500
		Production overhead (indirect materials)	4,200
		Selling & distribution overhead	500

Work in progress control

	£		£
January			
Stores ledger control (indirect materials)	34,500		

Production overhead control

	£		£
January			
Stores ledger control (indirect materials)	4,200		

Selling, Administration and Distribution Overhead

	£		£
January			
Stores ledger control	500		

3 Wages and salaries control

❑ The gross pay is debited to this account and credited to cost ledger control. It is then credited with the analysis figures from the coding of the payroll.

SUPPLYING INFORMATION FOR MANAGEMENT CONTROL

❏ **Example**

Tennis Skill Ltd gross pay for January 20X1 was £52,000. The analysis of the payroll from the coding system showed:

Direct labour	£37,500
Indirect labour	£4,500
Selling, distribution and admin salaries	£10,000

The control accounts would show:

Cost ledger control (CLC)

	£		£
		January gross pay	52,000

Wages and Salaries Control (WSC)

	£		£
January CLC	52,000	January W-I-P-C (direct labour)	37,500
		January Production overhead (indirect labour)	4,500
		January Selling and Distribution	10,000

Work in progress control (WIPC)

	£		£
January WSC	37,500		

Production overhead control

	£		£
January WSC	4,500		

Selling, Administration and Distribution Overhead

	£		£
January WSC	10,000		

❏ The actual cost analysis could be extracted from the system, and these figures would form part of the report of budget against actual elements of cost for various periods.

Notes

CHAPTER 10 BASIC BUDGETING AND STANDARD COSTING

1 Introduction to budgeting

❑ The nature of budgets

Budgets are plans set in financial and/or quantitative terms for either the whole of a business or for the various parts of a business for a specified period of time in the future. Budgets are prepared within the framework of objectives and policies that have been determined by senior management.

❑ Functions of budgetary control

The budgetary control process consists of two distinct elements:

- planning
- control

2 Preparing the budgets

This brings together a number of factors and also concerns various business sub-functions which include:

- Principal budget factor
    - sales demand
    - limitation of resources
- Sales budget
    - by volume and value
- Production budget
    - by products
- Raw materials
    - usage
    - cost of purchases
- Labour
    - direct
    - indirect
- Overheads
    - production
    - admin
    - selling and distribution

SUPPLYING INFORMATION FOR MANAGEMENT CONTROL

- Master budget
  - the operating statement comprising the sub-budgets shown above

❑ Conclusion

Budgetary control is a process whereby actual results are compared to budgeted figures and any significant differences must be investigated to discover the cause. Note that for Unit 4 you do not need to be able to prepare budgets, simply to compare budgeted figures to actual figures and to identify any discrepancies.

3 Example

See the eg, of Tennis Skill Ltd budget and actual labour cost by cost centre in Chapter 8, page 25

4 Standard costs

❑ Budgets are based on standard costs:

Standards

Definition

Standards are predetermined measurable quantities set in defined conditions.

A standard can be set for any activity. Suppose that a journey of 100 miles normally takes two hours. Then it could be said that the standard journey time was two hours. Equally it could be said that the standard speed on the journey was 50 miles per hour.

Standard cost

Definition

A standard cost is the cost expected for a single unit of output for a future period of time.

Standard costs are predetermined for direct labour, material and production overheads.

CHAPTER 10 BASIC BUDGETING AND STANDARD COSTING

❑ Conclusion

The function of budgetary control comprises the elements of planning and control.

Planning is the setting of realistic achievable targets, and control is the reporting and managerial action, resulting from the identification of variances for income and each element of cost.

CHAPTER 11   COMPARISONS OF INFORMATION

1   Introduction

This concerns dealing with comparisons of current actual costs with either those of a previous period or the budgeted (ie, planned) level of costs for the current period.

2   Current and previous period (actual)

The wages and salaries control account for Crescent Feeds Ltd showed:

W & S Control account

	£		£
January 20X1		January 20X1	
CLCA		(direct labour)	30,000
		Production overhead	6,500
		Admin overhead	1,000

W & S Control account

	£		£
February 20X1		February 20X1	
CLCA	40,000	W-I-P	34,000
		Production overhead	5,500
		Admin overhead	500

The production levels had been:
January   15,000 units
February   16,000 units

Present a comparison of the actual direct labour cost charged to work-in-progress for January and February, showing clearly the average cost of direct labour per unit of output and the cumulative cost for the year to date.

Notes

- Crescent Feeds Ltd

	January	Average cost per unit	**February**	Average cost per unit	**Total**	Average cost per unit
	£		£		£	
Direct labour	30,000		34,000		64,000	
Units of output	15,000	£2	16,000	£2.125	31,000	£2.06

3 Current period and budget

❑ Assume that for the two months ended February 20X1 Crescent Feeds Ltd budget showed:

Direct labour	£65,000
Indirect labour	£12,500
Admin salaries	£1,600
	£79,100

Budget production   30,000

Prepare a tabulation to show budget and actual labour costs for the period (two months ended February), showing clearly the increase or decrease in each element of labour cost and also a comparison of the total wages and salaries cost per unit for both the budget and actual performance.

Notes

SUPPLYING INFORMATION FOR MANAGEMENT CONTROL

Crescent Feeds Ltd

Wages and Salaries

Budget – Actual, January and February 20X1

	Budget	*Actual*	*(Increase)/ Decrease*	*Budget average cost per unit*	*Actual average cost per unit*
	£	£	£	£	£
Direct labour	65,000	64,000	1,000		
Indirect labour	12,500	12,000	500		
Admin salaries	1,600	1,500	100		
	79,100	77,500	1,600		
Production in units	30,000	31,000	1,000	2.64	2.50

Notes

CHAPTER 12 REPORTING

1 Introduction

❑ When communicating information which can range from an informal note through to a formal report, certain factors prevail and include:

- house style
- confidentiality.

2 Modes of communication

❑ The various modes of communication include:
- a note
- letter
- e-mail
- memorandum
- report.

- Note

    Probably the most simple and informal method of reporting information to another person in the organisation is by way of a note.

- Letter

    Format

    A letter should always have a letter heading showing the organisation's name, address, telephone number etc. Most organisations will have pre-printed letterheads for you to use.

    The letter must also be dated and the name and address of the recipient be included before the letter itself is started.

    The method of signing a letter will depend on the formality of how the letter begins.

    If a letter is started as 'Dear Sir' then the appropriate way to sign off the letter is 'Yours faithfully'.

Notes ◈ FOULKS*lynch*

However if the letter is started 'Dear Mr. Smith' then the appropriate way to sign off the letter is 'Yours sincerely'.

- E - mail

  An email must be addressed to the person to whom it is being sent using their e-mail address. It should also be given a title so that the recipient can see at a glance who it is from and what it is about.

  In terms of format of the content of the e-mail then there are no rules other than any organisational procedures that should be followed.

- Memorandum

  Definition

  A memorandum (or memo) is a written communication between two persons within an organisation. The plural of memorandum is memoranda.

  A memorandum serves a similar purpose to a letter. However the main difference is that letters are usually sent to persons outside the organisation, whereas memoranda or memos are for communication within the organisation itself.

  Format

  Many organisations will have pre-printed memo forms. In smaller organisations each individual may draft his own memoranda. However there are a number of key elements in any memorandum.

                                Memorandum

  To:

  From:

  Date:

  Ref:

  Subject:

CHAPTER 12 REPORTING

Body of memorandum

Signature:

Cc:

Enc:

Whatever the precise style and content of the memo, some general rules apply:

- there should be a heading to give an indication of the subject matter
- there should be an introductory paragraph setting the scene
- the main paragraphs of the memo should follow in a logical order, so that the recipient clearly understands the arguments being put forward
- there should be a summary of the main points.

- Reports

    Accountants are used to dealing with figures, but they must also learn to express themselves clearly in words. Accountants are (or should be) well prepared for the degree of precision and organisation required in report writing, but may need practice to improve their written style.
    Format
    The following guidelines for report writing should be observed:

- Reporting objectives

    Every report has several objectives. Generally these will be to:

    - define the problem
    - consider the alternatives

SUPPLYING INFORMATION FOR MANAGEMENT CONTROL

- make a reasoned recommendation for a specific alternative.

- Recipient

    The writer should consider the position of the recipient and design the report accordingly. Some recipients will require detailed calculations, others will have little time to study a lengthy report and should therefore be given one of minimum length consistent with providing the required information.

- Heading

    Each report should be headed to show who it is from and to, the subject and the date.

- Paragraph point system – each paragraph should make a point, each point should have a paragraph.

    This simple rule should always be observed. Important points may be underlined.

- Jargon and technical terms

    The use of jargon should be avoided at all times. If it is necessary to use technical terms, these should be fully explained, as should any techniques with which the recipient may be unfamiliar eg, decision trees, linear programming, marginal costing etc.

- Conclusion

    A report should always reach a conclusion. This should be clearly stated at the end of the report, not in the middle. The report should make it clear why you have arrived at the stated conclusion.

Notes

INDEX

Analysis of costs 5

Bar charts 27
Budgeting 36

Capital expenditure 21
Classification of costs 4
Code structure 10
Coding of costs and income 10
Collecting information 32
Communication 42
Comparisons of information 39
Controllable cost 4
Cost accounting 1
Cost bookkeeping 32
Cost centres 2, 20
Cost classification 4
Cost codes 10
Cost units 3

Data presentation 24
Depreciation 22
Diagram 25
Direct costs 4
Direct materials 15

E-mail 43
Expenses 20

Financial accounting 1

Graph 25

Incentive schemes 17
Interlocking accounts 32
Investment centres 3

Labour costs 16
Labour turnover 19
Letter 42

Management accounting 1
Management information 1
Material 13
Material costs 13
Memorandum 43
Multiple bar chart 28

Normal/abnormal costs 4
Note 42
Non-controllable cost 4

Overtime premium 19

Payroll 16
Pie charts 30
Prime cost 4
Profit centres 3

Recording of expenses 20
Remuneration methods 16
Reporting 42
Reports 44
Responsibility accounting 2
Revenue expenditure 21

Sales function 23
Selling function 23
Standard cost 37
Standard costing 36
Standards 37
Storekeeping 13
Stores ledger control 32

Tables 24

Use of computers 30

Wages 16
Wages and salaries control 33